I Can't Fly, But I Do.

By Benjamin Guthrie

With images by

Loring Baker

Edited by Maryann Ullman and Toby Shepherd

Copyright © 2010 Benjamin Guthrie

ISBN-13:
978-1540488145

ISBN-10:
1540488144

Dear Red,   March 2, 2018

    I hope this book treats you well. It comes from decent literary labor, and I hope that is evident. You might especially like "Impermanence" on pg 65.

        Love,
          Ben

Other works by the author:

66 Sayings
James, the Brave, Young Crow
The Parable of the Clingy Squirrels
Lift Up Your Voice

Dedication

To my late sister, Anne Guthrie (1981 – 2006), an ever-loving friend still inspiring my life these years later.

I Can't Fly, But I Do.

By Benjamin Guthrie

With Images by Loring Baker

Edited by Maryann Ullman and Toby Shepherd

Table of Contents

    I.   Love

A Thought-Filled Thought	14.
Easter Sunday	15.
A Musical Life	16.
But the Band Plays On	17.
Degas	18.
Leprosy	19.
Beethoven	20.
Signals	21.
She Didn't Have to Go	22.
Minimalism	23.
To Maria Callas	24.
Making Arcs	25.
Women	26.
Kindred Spirits	27.
During a Kiss	28.
I Supposed I Was Loving Her	29.
Taken Back	30.
Sing to Me	31.
Gone	32.
Clowns	33.
Weirdos	34.
Sahara	35.
3D Icon	36.

II.   Earth

A Well-Defined Mind	38.
Ars Poetica	39.
Heliolatry	40.
Helen Keller Thoughts	41.
Liberty	42.
Melodic Migration	43.
In the Oregon Wilderness	44.
Green Sings	45.
Counterintuition	46.
I Would Be that Tree	47.
Panentheism	48.
Taking On the Wind	49.
Impaired Imagination	49.
Revisiting a Cliché	50.
Sky Bums	51.
Lace	52.
Tactile Image	53.
The Tao of Evening	54.
Haiku 31	55.
There Is a Reason	56.
Airplanes	57.

III.   God

Looking Inside the Thought   59.
Oh Jesus, Man of Peace   60.
Wars and Rumors of War   61.
My God   62.
Stop   63.
In a Trance   64.
Impermanence   65.
Know Your Self   66.
People Forget   67.
The Illumination Chair   68.
Conundrum   69.
To Rise From the Dead   70.
Chance   71.
In This World   72.
Extravagance   73.
Streets Full of Bees   74.
Before a Jealous God   75.
The Fool   76.
Crucifixes   77.
Self-Expansion   78.
Silliness   79.
Christmas Reality   80.
Reverse Asceticism   81.

Biography   83.

Love

Eating My Mind ©2015, Loring Baker

Easter Sunday

"I am a worm, and not a man." –Psalm 22:6

If I loved you any more
than they think they love you,
I would tear you down
from all those crosses
shaming you there.

I would burn all crosses for your sake.

A Son of Man doesn't ask for worship,
especially as the image of a worm.

When a worm is so hung,
it has better posture.

They did spit on you,
but at least they didn't piss.

A Musical Life

When a child in church
rests his head on his mother's lap
and his ear to her belly,
he hears her singing quite well,
and she takes him to the memory
of the same sensation in utero.

There is a certain vibration
when she loves the hymn
and asserts enthusiasm:
his vision blurs,
and he enjoys it all the more,
even if her breathing is bouncy
and her belly is less soft.

But the Band Plays On

When your partner dies,
you might just quit dancing.
It's a mutual arrest
when she slumps there
in your arms.

The floor lacks a beat
when your feet are frozen.
You collapse together,
you wilt.

Degas

For John Berger

Ballerinas are the type
whose bare shoulder blades jut
like nubs to be wings.

Voyeurs like Degas are the type
that would know.

Some women like to so be watched,
at least by a lover or someone
of their private lives-

The arc of their backs bent in the shower,
the vanity in their eyes being painted
in the mirror.

I would be such a woman.
I want to share of my privacy.

Degas me.

Leprosy

To be without
and then forget:
to then be blind
in touch's sense.

To then be touched
with love's intent:
to flesh it out,
be more than mind.

To never know
love's touch is meant
to be its most
essential sign.

To have love leave
and so resign,
to wrongly think
your love is pent.

Beethoven

I thought this man pure storm
but then to hear those adagios
and how he so becomes the gentle giant.

A storm is supposed to be savage
and a giant a klutz.
What an irony then for serenity to flood
and a giant to nurse.

Signals

When a hand outstretched is cupped,
it is usually not to give.

When feet scurry in haste,
it is probably for fear.

A voice crying out
is normally to praise you.

She Didn't Have to Go

Her dead voice speaks-
a sort of sigh
full of language.

I hallucinate, and that is fine:
voices don't come from nowhere.
I hear myself speak in tongues-
a charismatic medium.

Even when you let go (and I have)
you still can't dive in
as they bury her
and let go of yourself.

Grandmothers die with their men
not trying to be Juliet.

Minimalism

I could wed you
for your eyes alone,
so I must be a Muslim.

I can guess
your obstructed smile
behind him dancing
and like it better
that way.

If I connect all the dots
the game will end,

and I love
how you play me.

To Maria Callas

Please speak plainly to me.
If you sing I get lost.

Forgive my forgetting language.

It's just I can't overhear your thoughts
when music's only word in English
is its own name.

Making Arcs

My hedonist friend said
he would love to die
on a maverick roller coaster
flown off the tracks.

His life would end in exhilaration.

I would like to be that old man
giving his last thrust when
his orgasm gives him a heart attack.

My eyes would roll back definitely.

Women

Women can seem just baby machines,
and what's sad is some want to be
and can't see past an animal fate.

For them freedom means to lack,
and a burden is a purpose.

I don't have this purpose.

Kindred Spirits

To inhabit one another,
and sometimes accidentally.
To find tameless gravity,
exponentially stronger
according to physical closeness
yet tactile dreams (when apart)
of breath on neck as in warm embrace.

To not let go at death
as though a herd of elephants
dragging with them ancestors' skulls,
oh what memories! as they plod.

A perpetual embrace of two trees
-branches interwoven-
seeming one totality
but of different stuff.

Then a wind spiral heaves,
about and together thrown:
clanking of the branch strands,
clapping of the trees' hands.
Then one uproots by the spiral,
hanging on for dear life lost.

A sort of mourning and a cherishing
like the elephants' dual rigor mortis grasp
-refusal to relinquish corpse of dead.

During a Kiss

You are all of this moment
but this moment is not all of you,
so you take many.

You are that flower in your hands,
only you are what it dreams to be.

You outlive it.

I Supposed I Was Loving Her

I supposed I was loving her
with that dress between us
until it fell to the floor
and her living whiteness
opened my mind like a scroll,

and that was just my eyes.

When each pore understood
that opening to another,
my mind became flesh
and I was outside myself
and then inside her.

Taken Back

I look into her drowning eyes
that sink behind themselves
but know she has no struggle
to her breathing since
its cloud of heat joins to mine
and I swim in there beside her
insuring we both are living
to the truest extent.

Sing to Me

Sing to me dear so I can dance.
Be the rhythm and the voice.

Open your mouth to love me this way.
I cannot be still in hearing such movement.

Gone

Two congruent walls of solid vines
in devotion clasp a lit house.

House darkens after years and dilapidates
since no one any longer lives there,

but vines still hold the negative space
of an empty embrace.

Clowns

We clowns wear masks to reveal our faces.
We don't hide behind the paint.
Her nose is bulbed and red from drinking.
His oversized shoes are his dad's and he can't fill them.
We fall without pain because so used to sincerity's discomfort.
We make slapstick of sadness and trudge the world along.
Don't be afraid of absurdity – he cries for no reason.

Weirdos

Many people
have a fetish
or two.

One strange guy
liked touching
pretty girls' feet
when bare or in sandals.

He always hid
in the college library
and would creep
under their desks.

Another had a thing
for touching hands
as he walked by girls
in the street.

If one looked him
in the eyes while passing
he would walk closely
and at the last minute
reach out almost behind him
to smooth his hand's back
to hers.

He always looked back
to see if they turned around.

Sahara

My mother's face is the type
that starving children dream of.

The very storm of sand which strips their bones
is that engraving her permanent smile.

Their barely ten years in time's sands
may be harder than her sixty of struggle,

but that dream outside time is a comfort
only found in such an image.

3D Icon

I wish we had a giant test tube
of formaldehyde fixed vertically
(with nice lights)
to hold her who's underground.

It would be a destination
for pilgrims like me,
set there in the corner
of her bedroom
(with nice lights).

We would trek there from wherever
and pause to look
and re-love her for a while.

What good is a coffin
in the first place?

I just want to see her.

Earth

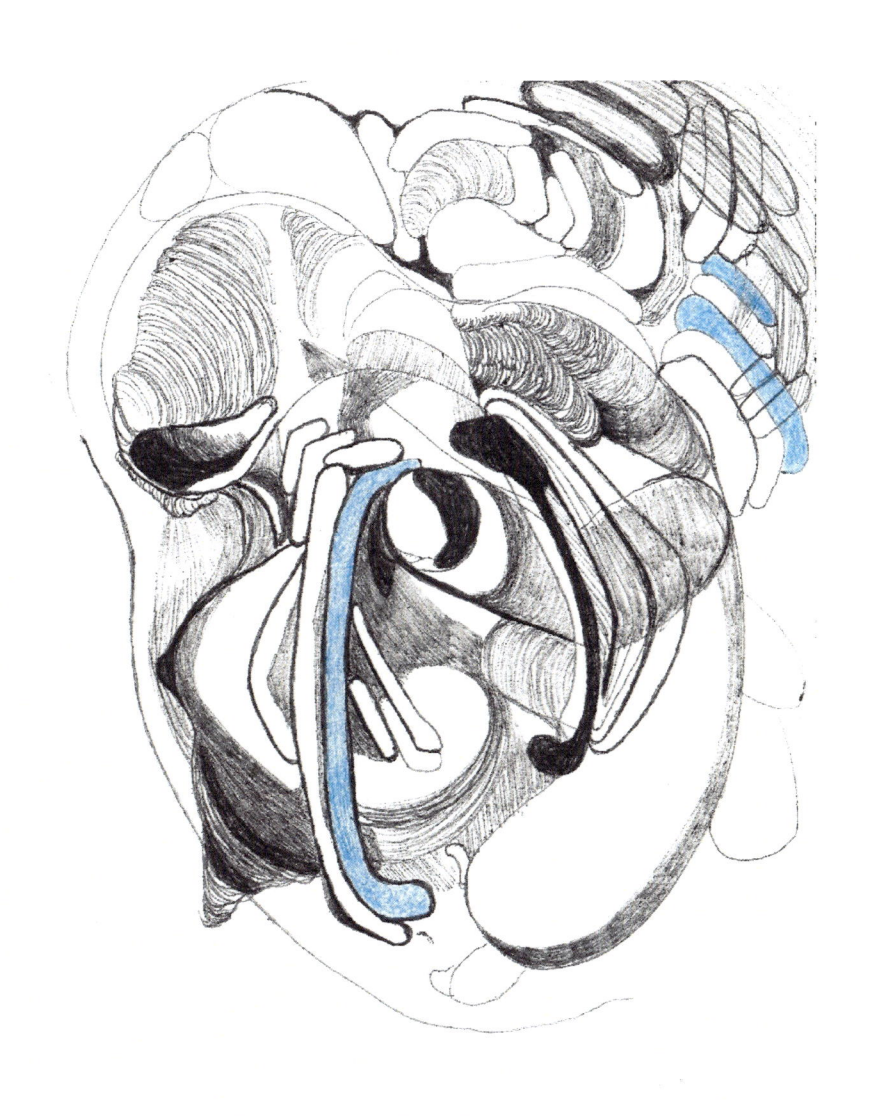

A Well-Defined Mind © 2015, Loring Baker

Ars Poetica

A river is not frozen in the winter-
it still is a moving thing.

The surface frozen is not the river,
and the force never hibernates.

And we must acknowledge
that the poem will never outdo the song:
the still season of poetry
pauses just a fraction of music's movement.

And we need not mourn the current quieting
of the poets-
it is only the river having a long summer.

Heliolatry

A sea bird holds his wings out
in stretched salute to the noon sun.

His beak is angled to it like a gentleman's.

A weathered woman does the same
with eyes shut to give a placid smile.

They both see sunsets behind their eyelids.

Helen Keller Thoughts

I live myself into all things.
I become water out of a glass,
water now no longer glass.
A glass of water is more than glass.

I the water become the sea,
a water much more than any glass.
Diffusing fresh into salt
I extend to floor and become the floor.

I the water and dirt grow into many things,
even mermaids.

Liberty

A man's dog is not a dog-
it's a man's dog.

There's a difference.

When it finds the sea
it forgets to be a man's.

Everything bound by that leash
then is more than free

because it never knows
how much it lacks liberty.

I can see how much
because I can smell my own as such.

Melodic Migration

Can the young bird but sing out of tune?
It seems an impossibility, though maybe.
She thrusts out in melody without wax or wane
in non-crescendo plainness, simplicity.
A tone without center or roof.
Is she not in truth without a home?

In the Oregon Wilderness

The almost sapling maples
find the patches of sunlight
in the forest and bloom there
like they have found their place
and are glad for it.

They send out these branches,
really stems that become
the shadows of the suspended leaves,
forever spring green,
in forever morning light,
each placed in uniform stance
but in random composition as a whole.

They're breathing parasols.

Green Sings

Green sings of what it means to be alive,
and life crescendos the dream
of what green means to be.

Green means to be music,
and music is dreams.

Life dreams green
and green lives to sing dreams.

Music is the green of life's dreams.

Counterintuition

It is strange
how the sea
from far away
can seem
a quietness,
as though
a well-seated
mountain
going nowhere.

When slightly audible,
the crash of waves
lacks in percussiveness
and seems gentle
like a drizzle of rain.

Even at shore,
the expanse
is so immense
that those waves
breaking at hand
seem a façade
to the stillness.

I Would Be that Tree

Each day is new for me
but much newer for a tree.

What augments it
will wither me.

A day is more real
if you better know
the sun is shining.

A tree thinks
of little else.

Panentheism

Surely the lilies feel a pleasure in their sex;
their mating surely has a special ritual.

A piece of their selves must be lost
to the wind that nests them in new ground.

The females must have drive to be mothers.

Are they not aware they are living?
They live with the purpose of exulting.

Taking On the Wind

The sloop departs the marina with sails down,
moving by gasoline and preparing for the wildness of the bay.

The sails rise with a sense of duty to do their job
and take on the wind.

With presumption the wind grabs the sails, leans the boat
and the gas engine continues to aid the movement, except
it's really just making noise and buzzing the boat.

But then the rush-
Captain Royce kills the buzz
and the effect is like jumping off a cliff-

There is nothing but wind.

Impaired Imagination

I never see animals
when I watch the clouds:
animals don't fly
with such magnitude
or so high;
neither do I see faces
nor anything real.

Instead, I see depictions
of the moments they share
of my life:

thoughts of coffee going down,
a song in my head,
memories of others' words,
my chatter in response.

Clocks merely measure
the prose of time.

Revisiting a Cliché

Why does the tear taste
anything like the sea?

The sea knows nothing
of sadness, and maybe not even joy-
except in testing its power
or in knowing the worlds it hides
from us inside itself.

The sea can only feel the indigestion
that is hubris.

The tear tastes something like the sea
so we can know how well it can drown us.

And there is thunder in that certain wail
or laughter.

Sky Bums

I wonder what reason seagulls have
to sit up there all day and drift around together?

Whole nations coast in the sky
as if with nothing to do
but be themselves in that certain pride
in what they don't do.

All their chatter is on how to keep in tune
with calculated wind patterns-
then how to contribute their patriotism
of idleness.

Lace

I learn intimacy
in the light of dawn
by grasping
its understatement
of touch without
wholly touching.

It's ballet's fantasy
and cashmere's ideal-

the essence of melon
and the gist of breeze.

It hums.

Tactile Image

The texture of wind:
like running your fingers across the surface
of wheat-like weeds of golden grass: impressions.
But not simply running them, rather
puttering (almost drumming) them along
like a gentle erotic massage.

The Tao of Evening

Before the night resumes its drone,
the light has a few last words
to conclude what it meant to say
in its monologue of daytime,

insisting to the Earth its intentions
are sincere as the instinct
to sing a child to sleep,

bowing with the dark to the Tao together
as they murmur their rites of dialogue
on how harmonic their vocal chords
can be together,

acquiescing to the night only after
having been assured the days Tao on.

Haiku 31

The loon takes in sun,
grabs two wings full, dives in sea,
spreads light under there.

There is a Reason

There is a reason birds have to sing:
it's because they can fly
and get past it all.

Birds go to heaven every day,
so they sing with euphoria.

But people sing with soul
and in suffering and somehow
go beyond them in song, for
soul is its own euphoria.

Airplanes

I can't fly, but I do.

My not flapping any wings
doesn't mean it's not happening.

A hummingbird can't walk, and it doesn't.
I am glad my legs are good for something.

I can cross the sky asleep.

God

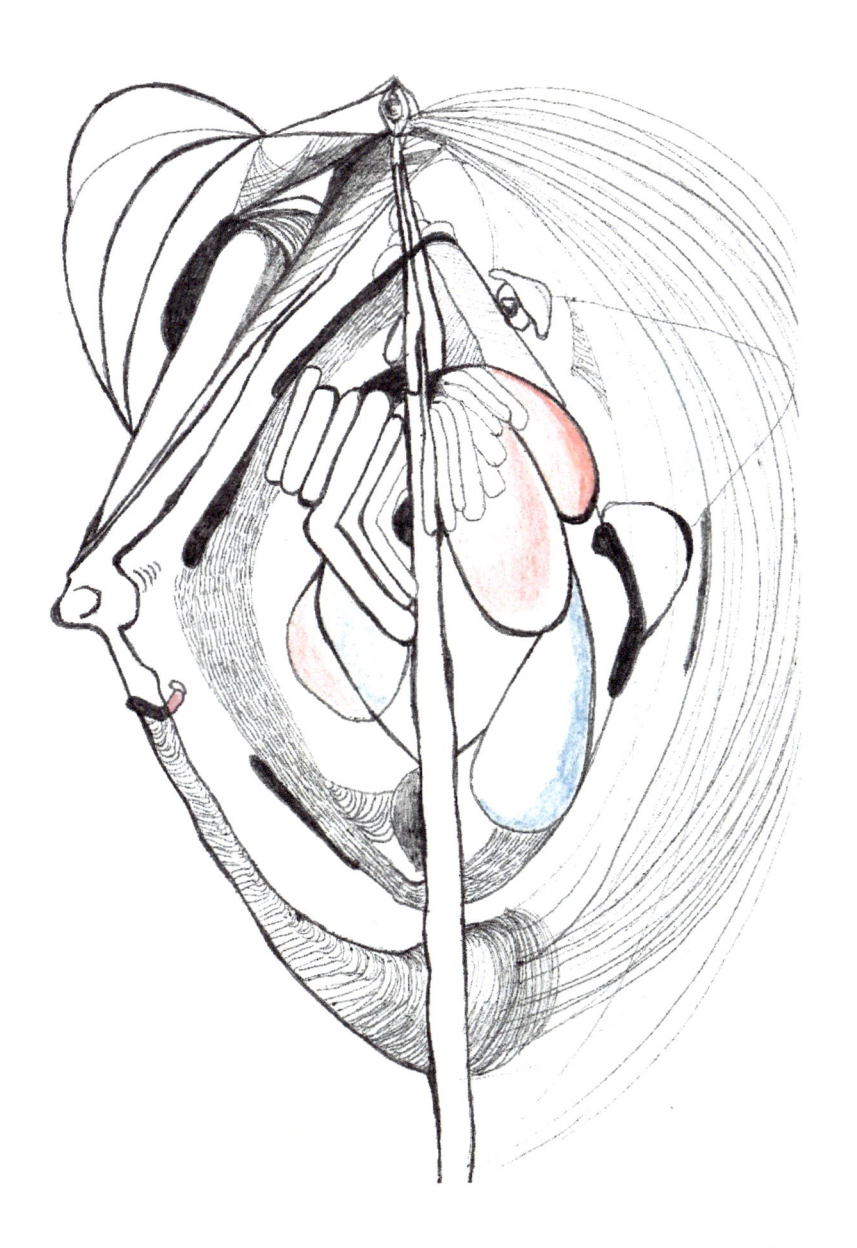

Looking Inside the Thought © 2015 Loring Baker

Oh Jesus, Man of Peace

Your words as you said are a sword,
much more vicious since your pen was dry.

Second hand, tenth hand—
enough hands to write
for two thousand years nonstop.

Mohammed had a working pen,
as did Moses and the others; how then
can the hand of God be limp?

Miracles only take so long.

To have a sword and not a pen
is less mighty and less tactful.

Shakespeare would have kissed your hand.

Wars and Rumors of War

When Allah met Yahweh
they fought at once over milk and honey.
They both knew they weren't alone
so that was nothing,
but they had different recipes
for their Jesus bread
and refused to divide the portions
or share the ingredients.

Krishna and Buddha were withdrawn
on a green tea diet and watched the scuffle
down in Death Valley from above in their mountain forest.
They would later wrestle on who could fast better.

The demon gods were under the table like dogs,
scrapping for crumbs from the feast.

The mortals followed suit to emulate their deities.

Jesus cried in the corner like a sissy
since he wanted his body back
and thought it was the answer.

My God

Your Peace is the suffering of suffering-
how little a kite suffers
when the wind breathes in tides.

Your Peace is how your Spirit fills-
how gently a boat can still be sailed
in a thick breeze.

Your Peace is how positive
a double negative can be-
how hard a windmill can work
by letting go.

Stop

You search for a light you won't find
till you swallow your eyes with your ears
and let the silence of darkness stop you to hear
what it means to be distracted.

To find light you must listen.

In a Trance

Because I am beautiful,
this moment is beautiful.

This moment makes me beautiful.

This moment is beautiful
because I am holding it
and letting it love me.

This moment is beautiful
because I let it hold me
and see that I am beautiful.

Impermanence

Bubbles and balloons
are round floating things
that kids chase around
for no reason
except giggles.

When a big bubble
gets blown, only it exists;
and when it pops
we still ponder it a while.

Balloons filled with breath
suspend themselves
and our attention in the air
like spacemen on the moon
or listening to music.

It's not hard
to relive this childhood-
all we need is to forget ourselves.

Know Your Self

Most windows look outside, not in.
Most want to know and not be known.

They see the world but not within:
the world is false when not within,
when good is veiled yet is your own.

People Forget

People forget what it means that we can fly.
It means we can leave the earth,
string smoke around it in a number of hours,
jump over the moon,
send mushroom clouds to crush whole cities,
melt the North Pole,
live the dreams we haven't had yet.

We can form new intelligence,
and then what are we?

The Illuminated Chair

After a long winter one day,
a Buddha saw the sun clear the sky
and he wanted to enjoy the light.

Because the night before had rained,
he wanted not to sit on the ground
in wetness, so he took a chair
to his lawn and sat down to sun.

When the chair felt his body warm
it began to share the heat,
and that heat soon made it glow.
The chair enjoyed the heat
but didn't know what it could do.

It was able to keep together
with all that force until the Buddha stood
as the sun went down, and it collapsed.

He laughed and cried to see it
because he so enjoyed the light
but also cared for his glowing chair.
He kept it with him, even if it was useless.

Conundrum

People hide themselves from cold fear
with the blanket assumption
that every question has an answer.

But if an answer is a question,
how is that an answer?

Mystery is the soul of question
and is no answer.
And when mystery darkens vision
fear grows colder,

but we can take only so much cold,

and we find no light or warmth
by hiding under more darkness.

To Rise from the Dead

He had to be a martyr.

They beat him like a slave
and hung him as a specimen.

His tomb rose him but not
in time to heal his wounds.

Clouds flew him away bleeding
to get him lost in space.

Where does a Jesus go
when going home?

Chance

All fires seemingly die
and many before
the wood is finished.

How lame to be a cinder
just sitting there.

But can we blame anyone?

The elements are enough
to extinguish all in a moment
but they sometimes also ignite.

I would I were a torch
lit by lightning, to be shared
with the snuffed.

In This World

I am a dove among sparrows.

I am more here because
there is more of me here,
and that more of me
better knows it.

The sparrows know less
of what yes means
and yes cares less
if they know.

A sparrow falls
and God takes note
yet only worms digest it,
but if I fall
great noise is made and
I am well-valued
in the mouths
who would take my life.

I have more life in me.

Extravagance

Oh Peace,

You are no white water
but I flood to know You.

You are a gong of whisper,
an un-scream, power's shadow.

You form me as a Canyon,
Grand from Your eons of stream.

Streets Full of Bees

A taxi can be a Bentley
but will still look like a taxi.

However plush the ride,
the fare will be the same.

He has to cart along any bastard
yet still may talk sincerely.

He must often find the brothel
and not at his chosen hour.

Oh that we were all like the taxi man
and stood on level footing.

Before a Jealous God

You whip yourself then prostrate,
begging pardon for delusional sins.

Your fault is contrition-
a face frozen to a marble floor.

You dream to outdo Jesus-
affliction is the beginning,
hungry lions an introduction.

He envies your paralysis-
your torture of ineptitude,
your anonymity.

To rise from prostration implies that
Yahweh remove his foot from your back.

The Fool

A man without books is a sad mind,
except that in much wisdom is much grief
and ignorance makes some people happy.

I would be happier knowing the grief.

The illiterate's thoughts become tragicomedy
when he escapes them because they aren't at hand
and written down.

He makes his whole world happier
because he knows so much less
of the many reasons to be sad.

He goes on unlearning their sadness.

Crucifixes

They walked the martyrs for days in the desert
to a high ravine that could be crossed with a bridge only.
To test them they made a crucifix their bridge,
so they had to walk on Christ to cross.

With guns in ribs, the martyrs chose to walk the cross
or jump the cliff. All but one chose to fall below.
That one refused to walk on Christ's face and stepped over it.
They shot him in the back once he made it.

The martyrs had also tested me out at sea.
They gave me shoes of bricks and tossed me in the deep
yet offered a crucifix to reach for rescue. I took the hold
and kept it in the boat so that when they let go

I held it upside down like a sword to beat them
with Christ's feet and knock them off the boat.
They were decent swimmers so they made it to land–
there's no use dying over trivialities.

Self-Expansion

I feared the dark as a child,
but only in closing my eyes to sleep
and seeing stars behind my eyelids
then galaxies passing by
and opening to bigger spaces.

Silliness

The 3-year-old
took her umbrella
in the shower:
she was tired of the drought-
it was her way to pray for rain.

Christmas Reality

Jesus was not some ornament
to keep nailed on those Easter trees.

And there weren't any Rabbits
laying eggs in mangers.

Would God really bleed so long there
mangled and prone to be speared
by any other Roman?

He makes a buffoon of godhood
but it's just his voice was that divine.

Reverse Asceticism

As a hermit to his cave
I retreat to my pleasures
and find home.
It is of the simplest questions
never asked,
Is not the flower blossoming
its heart's inversion?

About the Poet

Benjamin Guthrie was born in 1979 in Corpus Christi, Texas, as the first of five children to Greg and Mary Anne Guthrie, a conservative Christian couple from different parts of Texas. Growing up in a musical home, Benjamin's draw to literature came about cross-disciplinarily so that he continued to study it as such and earned an interdisciplinary diploma from Wheaton College, IL, where he combined the disciplines of music, literature, and art in a performance art show for his senior capstone. The issues of love, spirituality, music, and nature are very relevant to his worldview, which he is prolific to enumerate. Ever hungry for more life experience, he has furthered his studies in writing and music since and has traveled extensively so to find the truth of the world (as he sees it). In 2010, while in Buenos Aires, Argentina, he completed *I Can't Fly, But I Do.* but he has also published children's stories such as *James, the Brave, Young Crow* and *The Parable of the Clingy Squirrels*, both also available on Amazon.com.

Made in the USA
San Bernardino, CA
15 February 2018